# The Rock

## Pro Wrestler
## Rocky Maivia

by Michael Burgan

**Reading Consultant:**
Dr. Robert Miller
Professor of Special Education
Minnesota State University, Mankato

CAPSTONE
HIGH-INTEREST
BOOKS

an imprint of Capstone Press
Mankato, Minnesota

Capstone High-Interest Books are published by Capstone Press
151 Good Counsel Drive, P.O. Box 669, Mankato, Minnesota 56002
http://www.capstone-press.com

*Library of Congress Cataloging-in-Publication Data*
Burgan, Michael.
    The Rock: pro wrestler Rocky Maivia/by Michael Burgan.
    p. cm.—(Pro wrestlers)
    Includes bibliographical references (p. 45) and index.
    ISBN 0-7368-0918-X
    1. Rock (Wrestler)—Juvenile literature. 2. Wrestlers—United States—
Biography—Juvenile literature. [1. Rock (Wrestler) 2. Wrestlers.] I. Title. II. Series
GV1196.R63 B87 2002
796.812'092—dc21                                                          00-013076

Summary: Traces the personal life and career of professional wrestler Rocky Maivia.

**Editorial Credits**
Angela Kaelberer, editor; Lois Wallentine, product planning editor;
    Timothy Halldin, cover designer and illustrator; Katy Kudela, photo researcher

**Photo Credits**
Albert L. Ortega, 34
Al Messerschmidt/University of Miami, 19
Arnaldo Magnani/Liaison Agency, 38, 42
Dr. Michael Lano, 4, 6, 15, 17, 20, 23, 27
George De Sota/Liaison Agency, 30
Nancy Kaszerman/Zuma, 11
Reuters/Gary Hershorn/Archive Photos, cover inset (right); Reuters/Jim Bourg/
    Archive Photos, 40
Rich Freeda/WWF Entertainment/Liaison Agency, 12, 24
Steven E. Sutton/Duomo/CORBIS, cover, cover inset (left), 37
UPN/Liaison Agency, 28
WWF Entertainment/Liaison Agency, 32

1 2 3 4 5 6 07 06 05 04 03 02

Capstone Press thanks Dr. Michael Lano, WReaLano@aol.com, for his assistance in
the preparation of this book.

# Table of Contents

# Chapter 1

# A Champion Again

It was February 15, 1999. Wrestler Rocky Maivia stood inside the ring at Jefferson County Civic Coliseum in Birmingham, Alabama. Rocky was known as The Rock. He was about to wrestle Mick Foley. Foley wrestled under the name Mankind. The two men were competing for the World Wrestling Federation (WWF) World Championship.

Mankind was the current champion. He and Rocky had wrestled for the title in the past. Rocky had taken the title from Mankind twice. But Mankind took the title belt back

**Rocky is one of the WWF's top wrestlers.**

**Rocky has won the WWF World Championship a number of times.**

from Rocky on January 26, 1999. Rocky wanted to win the title one more time.

### Rocky Climbs the Ladder

The event was a ladder match. The belt hung from a wire above the ring. The wrestlers had to set up a ladder in the ring to reach the belt.

The first wrestler to climb the ladder and grab the belt would be the champion.

A special referee would oversee the match. This referee was wrestler Paul Wight. Wight is known as the Big Show.

The match began outside of the ring. Mankind attacked Rocky from behind. Rocky fought back. The wrestlers then entered the ring. Rocky dragged the ladder and a chair into the ring. Mankind set up the ladder and began to climb. Rocky then hit Mankind in the knee with the chair. Mankind fell to the mat as the ladder tumbled over on him.

During the match, Rocky used his signature moves. Rocky used the People's Elbow on Mankind. Mankind was on the mat. Rocky used his elbow to spear Mankind as he fell on top of him. Rocky also used the Rock Bottom. Rocky stood next to Mankind. He wrapped his arm around Mankind's head and neck. Rocky then picked up Mankind and slammed down his head and upper body. Mankind crashed through a table outside of the ring.

Rocky got back into the ring. He began to climb the ladder. Mankind followed him up the ladder's other side. Mankind used his signature move on Rocky. This move is the Mandible Claw. Mankind put a dirty sweat sock on his hand. The sock had a face drawn on it. Mankind called the sock "Mr. Socko." Mankind stuffed Mr. Socko in Rocky's mouth. Rocky fell off the ladder.

Mankind was just about to grab the belt. But the Big Show then entered the ring. He gave Mankind a chokeslam and pulled him off the ladder. Rocky climbed the ladder and grabbed the belt. Rocky was again the World Champion.

## About Rocky Maivia

Rocky Maivia is 6 feet, 5 inches (196 centimeters) tall and weighs 275 pounds (125 kilograms). His real name is Dwayne Johnson. People sometimes call him "The People's Champion" and "The Great One." Another nickname for Rocky is "The Brahma Bull." This breed of bull is famous for

# Major Matches

**November 16, 1996**—Rocky defeats Goldust at the Survivor Series.

**February 13, 1997**—Rocky defeats Triple H to win the WWF Intercontinental Championship.

**December 8, 1997**—Rocky again becomes the Intercontinental Champion after "Stone Cold" Steve Austin gives up the belt.

**November 15, 1998**—Rocky wins his first WWF World Championship by defeating Mankind.

**January 24, 1999**—Rocky defeats Mankind to win his second World Championship.

**February 15, 1999**—Rocky defeats Mankind to win his third World Championship.

**April 30, 2000**—Rocky defeats Triple H to win his fourth WWF World Championship.

**June 25, 2000**—Rocky wins the WWF World Championship for the fifth time.

**February 25, 2001**—Rocky defeats Kurt Angle to become the first six-time WWF World Champion.

There is a lot of Dwayne Johnson in
The Rock and a lot of The Rock
in Dwayne Johnson.
—Rocky Maivia, *WWF Magazine, The Rock
Special Collector's Issue*

being tough and strong. Rocky has a tattoo of
a Brahma bull on his right arm.

Rocky began wrestling in 1996. He won
his first major match on November 16, 1996.
In 1998, Rocky won his first WWF World
Championship. By 2001, Rocky had won
this title six times.

Rocky also is a Tag Team Champion. He
and Mankind have won the WWF Tag Team
title three times. Their team was called The
Rock and Sock Connection.

Rocky also is popular outside of the ring.
He has acted in TV shows such as *Saturday
Night Live, DAG*, and *That '70s Show*. He also
acted in the movie *The Mummy Returns*. In
2000, he published his autobiography. This
book tells the story of his life. It is called
*The Rock Says*.

In 2000, Rocky wrote a book about his life.

# Chapter 2

# The Early Years

Rocky was born May 2, 1972, in Haywood, California. His parents are Rocky and Ata Johnson. Rocky Johnson is from Nova Scotia, Canada. Ata Johnson is from Samoa. This group of small islands is located in the South Pacific Ocean.

Rocky Johnson was a professional wrestler. So was Ata's father. His name was Peter Maivia. As a boy, young Rocky often watched his father wrestle. Rocky Johnson traveled all over the United States to wrestle. Young Rocky sometimes practiced the moves his father used

**Rocky was born in Haywood, California.**

in the ring. Rocky also met many other professional wrestlers.

When he was 8, Rocky and his parents moved to Hawaii. His mother's parents lived there. Later, the Johnsons briefly lived in Connecticut and again in Hawaii. In 1987, the family settled in Bethlehem, Pennsylvania.

## Football Star

Rocky's family moved to Bethlehem when he was in 10th grade. Rocky attended Freedom High School in Bethlehem.

In 11th grade, Rocky joined the football team. Rocky played both tight end and defensive end. He was 6 feet, 4 inches (193 centimeters) tall and weighed 225 pounds (102 kilograms). He lifted weights for several hours each day to build his strength.

In 1989, Rocky had a great football season during his last year at Freedom High School. He had 14 sacks and more than 100 tackles. *USA Today* newspaper named him a high school All-American. Only the best football players in the United States win this honor.

**Rocky's parents are Rocky and Ata Johnson.**

Rocky wanted to play in the National Football League (NFL). But first, he needed to attend college. Several colleges showed an interest in offering Rocky a football scholarship. These schools included the University of Florida, the University of Miami, the University of Pittsburgh, and Clemson University. Rocky chose to play and study at the University of Miami.

## The Hurricanes

The University of Miami's football team is called the Hurricanes. The team usually is among the best in the United States. Rocky was not sure how much he would play as a freshman at Miami. Many first-year defensive linemen did not play at all. The school expected the freshmen only to train and practice.

Rocky's coaches were impressed with his skills. They wanted him to start playing right away. But Rocky's first season ended before the team played its first game. During a practice, he hurt his shoulder. He needed surgery to repair it. Rocky missed the entire 1990 season.

Rocky had other problems during his freshman year. He stopped attending classes. By December, school officials told Rocky that he would lose his scholarship if his grades did not improve. Rocky wanted to remain at the university and play for the Hurricanes. He started attending classes and studying each day. He also received extra help from a tutor. His grades soon improved. The school allowed him to keep his scholarship.

# The Rock's Heroes: Rocky Johnson and Peter Maivia

**Rocky Johnson and Rocky Maivia**

Rocky 's two most important wrestling heroes are his father and grandfather.

Rocky Johnson was a boxer, swimmer, and gymnast before he became a wrestler. He won Tag Team Championships in Canada, the National Wrestling Alliance (NWA), and the WWF. In the early 1980s, he won the WWF Intercontinental Championship. He retired from wrestling in the late 1980s.

Rocky Maivia's grandfather was High Chief Peter Maivia. To Samoans, a high chief is an important leader. During his career, Peter won a number of wrestling championships. Peter retired from wrestling in the 1970s. He died of cancer in 1982.

## Football Success

Rocky had a better season in 1991. He played in nine games and helped Miami win the 1992 Orange Bowl and a national championship.

The 1993 season was Rocky's best at Miami. He was one of the team's top defensive linemen. Some people thought he was one of the best in the country. He had six tackles during Miami's 49-0 victory over Syracuse University.

Rocky hoped to continue his success during the 1994 season. But he badly hurt his back during a practice. A doctor said that Rocky might never play football again. Rocky did not accept the doctor's opinion. He kept playing. Rocky spent most of the season in pain. He sometimes could not even undress himself after a game. The injury kept Rocky from playing well. He finally took two weeks off so his back could heal. Rocky felt and played better at the end of the season.

In 1995, Rocky graduated from the University of Miami. He earned a degree in criminology. He had the skills to be a police officer or a parole officer. He also thought about applying to be a Secret Service agent. These agents protect the

**Rocky had a successful football career at the University of Miami.**

president and other high-ranking U.S. government officials. But Rocky still wanted to play in the NFL. He was disappointed when no team drafted him. Rocky then received an offer to play football in Canada. In June 1995, Rocky joined the Calgary Stampeders of the Canadian Football League (CFL).

# Chapter 3

# Becoming a Wrestler

Rocky went to Calgary, Alberta, to play for the Stampeders. He trained hard. But he did not make the team. He was only a practice player. The Stampeders paid him to practice with the other players. Rocky barely made enough money to eat. He lived in a small apartment with three other practice players. They slept on mattresses that a local motel had thrown in the trash.

In October 1995, the Stampeders let Rocky go. The Stampeders' coach told Rocky that he could try out for the team again the next year.

**Rocky decided to become a wrestler after failing to make the Calgary Stampeders football team.**

But Rocky decided he did not want to play in the CFL. Instead, he thought about becoming a professional wrestler. Rocky called his father to tell him about his plan. Rocky Johnson was upset. He did not want his son to wrestle. He knew how difficult a wrestler's life could be. But Rocky had made up his mind. His father agreed to teach him how to wrestle.

### Learning to Wrestle

Rocky went with his father to a gym in Tampa, Florida. Rocky worked with his father and a wrestler named Ron Slinker. Rocky practiced basic wrestling moves such as lockups and headlocks. He also continued to lift weights to build up his muscles.

Rocky trained for several months. He then called Pat Patterson. Patterson once wrestled with Rocky's grandfather. He now worked for the WWF. Rocky hoped to impress Patterson with his skills. Patterson agreed to watch Rocky wrestle.

Patterson liked how Rocky wrestled. He called Vince McMahon. McMahon owns the

**Before joining the WWF, Rocky lifted weights to build up his muscles.**

WWF. He agreed to give Rocky a tryout in Corpus Christi, Texas. If Rocky wrestled well, he had a chance to join the WWF.

At the tryout, Rocky decided to use his real name. He wrestled as Dwayne Johnson. His first opponent was Steve Lombardi. Lombardi is known as the Brooklyn Brawler. Rocky won this first match.

**Rocky impressed WWF officials with his wrestling skills.**

Rocky had another tryout the next night. He
wrestled Chris Candido. This time, Rocky lost
the match. But McMahon and the WWF liked
how Rocky performed. They offered him a
contract. Rocky became a professional wrestler.
But he still needed more training. The WWF

asked him to wrestle first in the United States Wrestling Alliance (USWA). This organization was located in Memphis, Tennessee.

## Reaching the WWF

Some sports have minor leagues. Players improve their skills in the minor leagues before they join a major professional team. The USWA was similar to a minor league. Wrestlers in the USWA learned more about wrestling before joining the WWF.

Rocky wrestled in the USWA for a few months in 1996. He called himself Flex Kavana. He wrestled at fairgrounds and inside barns for $40 each night.

In the fall of 1996, the WWF asked Rocky to come to Stamford, Connecticut. The WWF has a gym there where the top wrestlers train. Rocky knew that the invitation to Stamford meant that the WWF liked how he wrestled.

The WWF gave Rocky his first real match on November 16, 1996. It also gave him a new name. McMahon wanted Rocky to use his father's first name and his grandfather's last name. The name would show fans that Rocky came from a great wrestling family. Rocky agreed to wrestle as Rocky Maivia.

Rocky's first match was at the Survivor Series at New York City's Madison Square Garden. The arena was filled with almost 20,000 fans. Rocky wrestled with seven other wrestlers in one match. All of the other wrestlers were well known. Rocky and Dustin Runnels were the last two men in the ring. Runnels wrestled as Goldust. Rocky pinned Goldust to the mat and held him down for the three-count. Rocky's win meant that he was about to become a WWF star.

**Rocky won most of his early WWF matches.**

# Chapter 4

# WWF Star

All professional wrestlers play a role during their matches. Some are mean to their opponents and the fans. These wrestlers are known as "heels." Other wrestlers are heroes. They are called "babyfaces" or "faces."

Rocky began his WWF career as a babyface. He always smiled and acted happy. In February 1997, Rocky became the WWF Intercontinental Champion. He defeated Paul Levesque for the title. Levesque is known as Hunter Hearst Helmsley or Triple H. But many fans did not like Rocky. They often booed him when he entered the ring. One night, Rocky saw a fan holding a

**Rocky began his career in the WWF as a babyface.**

**Rocky enjoyed the role of a heel as The Rock.**

sign. The sign said, "Die, Rocky, die."
Soon, fans brought these signs to all of
Rocky's matches.

In April 1997, Rocky lost his
Intercontinental belt to Owen Hart. He also
injured his knee. He returned to the ring in
August. The WWF wanted Rocky to become a
heel. He agreed. Rocky was tired of playing a
babyface and being booed. Rocky joined a

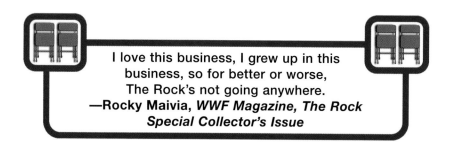

> I love this business, I grew up in this business, so for better or worse, The Rock's not going anywhere.
> —Rocky Maivia, *WWF Magazine, The Rock Special Collector's Issue*

group of wrestlers called the Nation of Domination. All of the Nation's members were heels.

## Becoming The Rock

Rocky became a more violent wrestler as a heel. The crowds booed him even more than before. But Rocky did not mind the boos. He enjoyed his new role. In December 1997, he challenged "Stone Cold" Steve Austin to a match. Austin was one of the most popular wrestlers in the WWF. He also was the Intercontinental Champion. Rocky said that he would beat Austin. He also called himself "The Rock" for the first time.

On December 7, Rocky and Austin wrestled in Springfield, Massachusetts. Rocky used the People's Elbow on Austin. He also threw a punch. But the punch missed its target. Austin then used his signature move on Rocky. This move is called the Stone Cold Stunner. Austin

**Rocky wore expensive clothes and sunglasses as part of his new character.**

stood in front and slightly to the side of Rocky. He wrapped his arm around Rocky's head. He then dropped to his knees as he slammed Rocky to the mat.

The next night, Vince McMahon wanted Austin and Rocky to wrestle again. Austin refused. He gave the Intercontinental belt to Rocky. Rocky soon had a new nickname. He called himself "The People's Champion."

Rocky was still a heel. As The Rock, he acted like he was the best wrestler in the world. He wore expensive clothes and sunglasses. The Rock made fun of other wrestlers and the fans. He called them "jabronis." Rocky learned this word from his father and other older wrestlers. It means a useless or stupid person.

Fans began to like The Rock. They also began to use the word "jabroni." The Rock used other sayings. He asked fans, "Do you smell what The Rock is cooking?" He meant, "Do you understand what I'm saying?" The Rock also raised one eyebrow when he talked to the fans. He called this expression "The People's Eyebrow." Rocky once again became a babyface. But this time, the fans cheered for him.

## WWF World Champion

In August 1998, Rocky lost his Intercontinental title to Triple H. But on November 15, Rocky wrestled for the WWF World Championship. This match took place at the Survivor Series in St. Louis, Missouri. At this match, Rocky wrestled and beat Ray Traylor, Ken Shamrock, and Mark Calloway. Traylor wrestles as the Big

Rocky has wrestled against most of the top WWF wrestlers. But some of his best matches have been against "Stone Cold" Steve Austin.

Steve Austin is 6 feet, 2 inches (188 centimeters) tall and weighs 252 pounds (114 kilograms). His real name is Steve Williams. His signature move is the Stone Cold Stunner.

Like Rocky, Austin played football in college. He played for North Texas State University. This school now is called the University of North Texas.

Austin began wrestling in Texas in 1989. He wrestled for World Class Championship Wrestling (WCCW). He also wrestled for World Championship Wrestling (WCW) and Extreme Championship Wrestling (ECW). He joined the WWF in 1995. Austin has won the WWF Championship five times and the WWF Intercontinental Championship twice.

Boss Man. Calloway is the Undertaker. The last match was against Mankind. Rocky took Mankind's arms and legs and twisted them. Mankind yelled in pain. He quit the match. At 26, Rocky was the youngest wrestler ever to win the World Championship. The next night, he defended his title against Steve Austin. Rocky remained the World Champion.

Rocky often wrestled Mankind during the next few months. On December 29, Mankind defeated Rocky at a match in Worcester, Massachusetts. On January 24, 1999, Rocky won the belt again at the Royal Rumble in Anaheim, California. On January 26, Mankind defeated Rocky at a match in Tucson, Arizona. But Rocky regained the belt on February 15 in Birmingham, Alabama.

Rocky then prepared to defend his title at WrestleMania. This event took place on March 28 in Philadelphia, Pennsylvania. Rocky's opponent was Steve Austin.

Rocky's match at WrestleMania lasted almost 30 minutes. He used the Rock Bottom on Austin. Austin responded with a Stone Cold Stunner. Rocky fell to the mat but was able to get up.

Vince McMahon entered the ring to try to help Rocky. Mankind ran into the ring and knocked out McMahon. Rocky then used the Rock Bottom and the People's Elbow on Austin. But Austin got up again. Austin then used the Stone Cold Stunner to pin Rocky. Austin was the new WWF World Champion.

## Champion Again

Rocky was no longer the World Champion. But he remained popular with the fans. He sometimes wrestled with Mankind in tag team matches. On August 30, 1999, they won their first Tag Team Championship. During that match, they defeated the Big Show and the Undertaker. They won the title two more times later that year.

On April 30, 2000, Rocky wrestled Triple H for the WWF World Championship. During the match, the referees helped Triple H. McMahon also helped by hitting Rocky with a chair. Steve Austin then came out to help Rocky. Austin hit McMahon, Triple H, and the referees with a chair and then left the ring. Rocky used the People's Elbow on Triple H

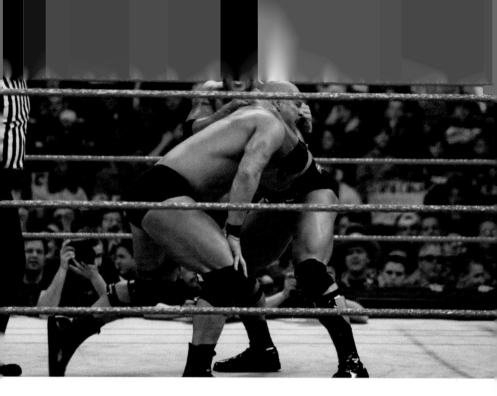

On March 28, 1999, Rocky wrestled Steve Austin for
the WWF World Championship.

and then pinned him. Rocky was once again
the World Champion.

In May, Rocky and Triple H met in an Iron
Man match. Rocky and Triple H wrestled for
one hour. They tried to pin each other as often
as they could. Triple H ended with six pins.
Rocky had five. Triple H was again the World
Champion. But Rocky knew that he would have
another chance to win back the belt.

# Chapter 5

# Rocky Maivia Today

Rocky continues to be one of the best wrestlers in the WWF. On June 25, 2000, Rocky won the World Championship for the fifth time. But he lost the title on October 22 to Kurt Angle.

On February 25, 2001, Rocky again wrestled Angle for the title. The match took place at No Way Out in Las Vegas, Nevada.

Rocky defeated Angle. Rocky then became the first wrestler to win the WWF World Championship six times.

**Rocky often shows fans "The People's Eyebrow."**

In 2000, Rocky spoke at the Republican National Convention in Philadelphia, Pennsylvania.

## Life Outside the Ring

On May 3, 1997, Rocky married Dany Garcia. Dany and Rocky met at the University of Miami. They live in Davie, Florida. Dany works as a vice president for a financial company. Rocky does not spend much time at his home. He travels about 225 days each year. Rocky spends time with Dany and his parents when he is not working.

Rocky sometimes makes special
appearances. He works for charities
such as the Make-a-Wish Foundation.
This organization helps children who are
seriously ill. In 2000, Rocky spoke at the
national conventions of the Democratic and
Republican parties. At the conventions, these
political parties selected who would run for
U.S. president and vice president. Rocky's
speeches encouraged young people to vote.

Rocky has appeared on TV shows. On
*That '70s Show,* he played the role of his father,
Rocky Johnson. In March 2000, Rocky hosted
*Saturday Night Live.* Later that year, Rocky
appeared as himself on the TV show *DAG.*

Rocky also has acted in movies. He played
a character called the Scorpion King in *The
Mummy Returns.* In March 2001, Rocky began
work on another movie about the Scorpion
King. Rocky enjoys acting in movies. But he
also plans to continue his wrestling career.

**41**

# Career Highlights

**1972**—Rocky is born May 2 in Haywood, California.

**1989**—*USA Today* names Rocky a high school All-American football player.

**1991–1994**—Rocky plays football for the University of Miami.

**1996**—Rocky signs a contract with the WWF, wrestles for the United States Wrestling Alliance, and wins his first WWF match.

**1997**—Rocky wins the WWF Intercontinental Championship.

**1998**—Rocky wins his first WWF World Championship.

**1999**—Rocky wins his first WWF Tag Team Championship.

**2000**—Rocky wins the WWF World Championship for the fifth time. He also publishes an autobiography called *The Rock Says*.

**2001**—Rocky becomes the first six-time WWF World Champion.

# Words to Know

**autobiography** (aw-toh-bye-OG-ruh-fee)—a book in which the author tells the story of his or her life

**criminology** (krim-uh-NAH-luh-jee)—the scientific study of crime

**jabroni** (jah-BROH-nee)—a wrestling term for a useless or stupid person

**opponent** (uh-POH-nent)—a person who competes against another person

**referee** (ref-uh-REE)—a person who makes sure athletes follow the rules of a sport

**scholarship** (SKOL-ur-ship)—a grant of money that helps a student pay for education costs

**signature move** (SIG-nuh-chur MOOV)—the move for which a wrestler is best known; this move also is called a finishing move.

**tutor** (TOO-tur)—a teacher who gives private lessons to one student at a time

# To Learn More

**Alexander, Kyle.** *Pro Wrestling's Most Punishing Finishing Moves.* Pro Wrestling Legends. Philadelphia: Chelsea House, 2001.

**Burgan, Michael.** *Stone Cold: Pro Wrestler Steve Austin.* Pro Wrestlers. Mankato, Minn.: Capstone High-Interest Books, 2002.

**Greenberg, Keith Elliot.** *Pro Wrestling: From Carnivals to Cable TV.* Minneapolis: Lerner, 2000.

**Ross, Dan.** *The Rock: The Story of the Wrestler They Call "The Rock."* Pro Wrestling Legends. Philadelphia: Chelsea House, 2001.

# Useful Addresses

**Extreme Canadian Championship Wrestling**
211 20701 Langley Bypass
Langley, BC  V3A 5E8
Canada

**World of Wrestling Magazine**
Box 500
Missouri City, TX  77459-9904

**World Wrestling Federation
    Entertainment, Inc.**
1241 East Main Street
Stamford, CT  06902

# Internet Sites

**Canadian Pro Wrestling Hall of Fame**
http://www.canoe.ca/SlamWrestling/
    hallofame.html

**Professional Wrestling Online Museum**
http://www.wrestlingmuseum.com/home.html

**The Rock.com**
http://www.therock.com

**WWF.com**
http://www.wwf.com

# Index